D1137191

ESSENTIAL

WRITING
SKILLS

LONDON, NEW YORK, MUNICH,
MELBOURNE, DELHI

Senior Editor Jacky Jackson
Senior Art Editor Sarah Cowley

DTP Designer Rajen Shah
Production Controller Michelle Thomas

Managing Editor Adèle Hayward
Managing Art Editor Karen Self

ST. HELENS
COLLEGE

O 004043
JAC

116974

July 06

LIBRARY

First published in Great Britain in 2002 by
Dorling Kindersley Limited,
80 Strand
London, WC2R 0RL

A Penguin Company

4 6 8 10 9 7 5

Copyright © 2002 Dorling Kindersley Limited
This edition was adapted from a Brazilian book by José
Paulo Moreira de Oliveira and Carlos Alberto Paula Motta
Text © 2000
Previously published by Publifolha Edifício Jatobá © 2000

All rights reserved. No part of this publication may be
reproduced, stored in a retrieval system, or transmitted in
any form or by any means, electronic, mechanical,
photocopying, recording, or otherwise, without the prior
written permission of the copyright owner.

A CIP catalogue record for this book is available
from the British Library

ISBN 0 7513 3364 6

Reproduced by Colourscan, Singapore
Printed in China by WKT

See our complete catalogue at
www.dk.com

CONTENTS

4 INTRODUCTION

WRITING EFFECTIVELY

6 COMMUNICATING
CLEARLY

8 DEVELOPING WRITING
SKILLS

10 RECOGNIZING GOOD
WRITING

12 PREPARING TO
WRITE

16 DEFINING YOUR
STYLE

Understanding the Basics

22 Taking the First Steps

24 Composing Good Sentences

26 Using Different Voices

30 Knowing the Rules

34 Presenting Your Work

38 Writing Positively

40 Communicating with the Reader

Structuring Your Writing

42 Establishing Procedures

46 Using the Inverted Pyramid

48 Writing Business Reports

50 Using Questions and Answers

52 Identifying Problems and Proposing Solutions

Using Everyday Formats

54 Writing Letters

58 Writing E-mails

60 Composing Direct Mail Letters

62 Presenting Business Reports

66 Assessing Writing Skills

70 Index

72 Acknowledgments

INTRODUCTION

Knowing how to communicate effectively through writing is essential for anybody who wants to progress in today's competitive business environment. Writing Skills is a valuable tool that will help you meet that challenge. It is divided into four parts, each outlining key requirements for good writing: a clear and concise style, knowledge of grammar and structure, and how to apply basic formats to everyday communication. It also shows how to project the right image, choose the kind of language best suited to your reader, and write succinct e-mails, reports, and letters.

Information and advice are given that will help you to become a skilled communicator. In addition, 101 concise tips highlight the secrets of good writing, and a self-assessment test at the end of the book will enable you to evaluate the progress you have made.

WRITING EFFECTIVELY

In this age of mass information and communication, being able to write clearly is fundamental to business success. Crucial decisions may depend on the written word in letters, reports, and e-mails.

COMMUNICATING CLEARLY

Knowing how to communicate efficiently in the current employment market is an enormous competitive advantage. The ability to take on board, change, and process information – mostly in written form – is a formidable business skill.

> **1** A clear style projects an efficient image, so choose words carefully.

> **2** For electronic communications, always write in a simple language.

> **3** Writing positively and directly can influence and motivate others.

WRITING IN A PROFESSIONAL WAY

The written word projects your professional image to your boss, colleagues, clients, and suppliers. Your values, beliefs, ideologies, and personality all come through in the material that you produce. And it does not end there. Your knowledge, training, education, organizational skills, and creativity are also shown in the words you use and how you convey information. This information must be credible and supported by facts, because the people receiving it must have confidence in you and what you have written.

Changing Old Beliefs

Many professionals feel that writing is an old-fashioned form of communication. But in this electronic age, writing is a day-to-day necessity, and perhaps even more important than ever before. Another belief that needs to be corrected is that it is not possible to write inspirational text. With the right skills, methods, models, and lots of practice, everyone can write creatively. A third belief is that it is the quality of the writing that is important, not how it is read and received. The fact is that if a communication is badly written, it will not be clearly understood by its recipient, particularly if they are unfamiliar with, or do not have, in-depth knowledge of the subject matter.

Updating Methods

In many established companies, old-fashioned or bureaucratic methods or styles of communication are often used, which can hinder rather than promote clear understanding between colleagues or suppliers. Memos or letters using an outmoded structure, or templates with pedantic or convoluted language are often used, which can sometimes confuse the recipients. But all of us can become involved in suggesting how to change and improve these old-fashioned methods and styles, so that clear, concise writing becomes the main form of communication.

The aim is to produce communications that are well-written, interesting to read, and which will motivate and inspire.

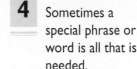

4 Sometimes a special phrase or word is all that is needed.

5 Learn how to use the most up-to-date methods of communication.

▼ USING NEW TECHNOLOGY
The electronic age enables us to take a laptop computer with us anywhere. You can work on a train, at someone else's desk, or make notes in a meeting.

DEVELOPING WRITING SKILLS

To understand the importance of written language and the best way to use it, it is helpful to know something about how we write. Nowadays, with the speed of electronic communication, all text needs to be brief and focused.

6 Write all informal communications in a modern, lively style.

POINTS TO REMEMBER

- Written language is increasingly important in today's business.
- Direct mail lists, databases, and the internet are strategic activators and motivators in business operations.
- E-mail is becoming an extremely important tool, often replacing phone contact because of its speed and the records it provides.
- Written information is often circulated before filing, so extra care needs to be taken with text presentation.

WRITING THROUGH THE AGES

Society has moved through three major stages: the agricultural age, the industrial age, and now the electronic age (also known as the information age). Each period has brought changes in the methods and styles in which people communicated for business. The most recent and significant change in our current information age has been a transition from the more formal business language of the past to the informal approach used today, particularly in e-mails.

An electric keyboard for easier and faster typing

▶ **TECHNOLOGICAL DEVELOPMENTS**
How we impart information has changed over the years, from using a basic manual typewriter through a faster electric version to the modern computer where people write directly "on screen."

Manual keys

MANUAL TYPEWRITER

ELECTRIC TYPEWRITER

USING VISUAL SKILLS

For today's young generation, highly visual resources such as television, the Internet, video games, and multimedia resources are part of their normal day-to-day life. The visual presentation of materials as a business aid is also becoming increasingly important. Try using schematics – classifying information under specific headings alongside other visual aids, such as graphics, tables, charts, and colour. These can all be applied to the material to make its presentation more interesting and focused.

 7 With large sections of text, use headings and boxes to break them up.

8 Reduce information overload by restricting the text on each page.

TARGETING YOUR MATERIAL

In modern business communications, the written material that is sent out must be targeted carefully. For example, in a letter to an interested party, you must state clearly what benefits there are to the consumer of your products and services, rather than just describing them. Present all the information in a clear, simple, but dynamic style using persuasive terminology, that will capture the client's attention.

A screen for faster text changes

New machines come with diverse functions, are quicker, and have more memory

Basic word processing

OLD COMPUTER

MODERN COMPUTER

RECOGNIZING GOOD WRITING

All business professionals need to become good communicators to succeed. To do this, it is essential to recognize, and correct, any bad or lazy writing habits that have developed, and establish good habits such as organization and focus.

> **9** In day-to-day business, adopt a friendly but elegant style.

> **10** When supplying information, keep to the points you are trying to make.

▼ CHANGING WAYS OF WORKING
There are marked differences between how a bad and good communicator operates, but it is possible to change negative ways of working into positive ones.

GETTING ORGANIZED
Good commmunicators are easy to identify because they get themselves organized before they write any material. They research the subject matter to be discussed, and have defined objectives to motivate their readers to action. They always consider what information the reader needs, and review and rework their written work for increased clarity and sense. Bad communicators write in a hurried, disordered way without any prior thought or planning. They leave the reader to work out what they are trying to say.

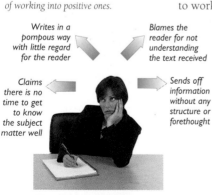

Writes in a pompous way with little regard for the reader

Blames the reader for not understanding the text received

Claims there is no time to get to know the subject matter well

Sends off information without any structure or forethought

THE BAD COMMUNICATOR

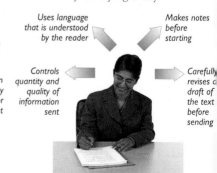

Uses language that is understood by the reader

Makes notes before starting

Controls quantity and quality of information sent

Carefully revises a draft of the text before sending

THE GOOD COMMUNICATOR

FOCUSING YOUR WRITING

When writing your text, be focused about what message you are trying to get across. In a marketing letter, for example, present the information in a punchy, positive style to encourage the maximum reader response. Be careful not to obscure your message with a dull and pedantic writing style.

11 Check the tone of your text by reading it out loud.

◀ WRITING WITHOUT FOCUS

This marketing letter contains the information about the Small Business Programme at Zedcom, but it is not written or presented in a style that projects it positively to the reader. The text comes across as stilted and bland, leaving the reader with no desire to join Zedcom.

31 March 2000

Subject: Small Business Programme at Zedcom

Dear Sir,

The Small Business Programme at Zedcom aims to offer all participants the unique opportunity to set up and manage their own business.

All participants will receive essential information on the management and marketing of products, price setting, quality and stock control, and the training of colleagues, as well as learning other management skills.

Zedcom hopes through this initiative to offer participants, at no expense to themselves, increased opportunities, income, and an improved standard of living.

If this programme interests you, information can be obtained by telephoning 0800 000000.

WRITING WITH FOCUS ▶

This marketing letter has been planned well. It advertises the programme run by Zedcom, selling its merits to the reader in a short and punchy style. The focus is on the reader, and the text is broken up into accessible paragraphs.

ARE YOU SEEKING NEW OPPORTUNITIES, MORE MONEY, AND A HIGHER STANDARD OF LIVING?

If this is what you are looking for, then take part in the Small Business Programme – a new initiative run by Zedcom.

The programme will teach you how to start up and run your own business.

You'll learn, in a simple and practical way, how to:
✔ manage and market products
✔ work out pricing levels
✔ improve the quality of products and services
✔ control stock
✔ train and involve colleagues

You will also learn basic management skills and techniques.

The programme is free of charge, so call 0800 000000 to register your place now.

Don't miss out – this is just the opportunity you have been waiting for.

PREPARING TO WRITE

A good writing style has several different elements. It should give a positive message, show the writer's familiarity with the subject matter, relate the right information in a concise, friendly manner, and, if necessary, motivate the reader.

12 Always write in terms that your reader can understand.

ASSESSING YOUR STYLE

UNHELPFUL "We are not able to assist you…"	or	**CO-OPERATIVE** "We are willing to look at…"
UNDERMINING "I am not sure you can do this job…"	or	**SUPPORTIVE** "I think you are doing this job well…"
AUTHORITARIAN "You must complete this job now…"	or	**DEMOCRATIC** "When you have time, could you…"
ABRUPT "Well, if you cannot handle the project…"	or	**PERSUASIVE** "I really think this is your project…"
POMPOUS "I have worked on many jobs like this…"	or	**UNASSUMING** "I will do my best on this job…"

PROJECTING THE RIGHT IMAGE

The style and tone that you use for writing project your image, and can also reflect your credibility in the workplace. They give an indication of your personality and confidence in yourself in the work environment. A letter or e-mail that is written in an abrupt or unhelpful style will not inspire a client or colleague to respond as you wish – they are far more likely to reply in a similar vein. Using a persuasive or co-operative tone will instantly engage the recipient, making them much more likely to respond in a positive, helpful manner. The way someone reacts to the tone of a letter is very personal, but always try to be clear, objective, and polite in everything you write.

13 Plan carefully what you want to say and do a rough version.

PLANNING YOUR WORK

Before you start writing, structure a plan of what you are trying to say: this can be in note or bullet form. If you do not know what your objectives are, the people receiving your communication will also be confused and wonder what you need from them. A good piece of writing conveys the intended message with clearly defined objectives so that the recipients respond positively and take the necessary action. Make the text clear and precise, so that they know what decisions are required of them, and detail any time scale that is involved.

Well-structured text is fundamental to achieving good communication with any client

USING THE RIGHT LANGUAGE

When you are writing to clients or associates, you will need to vary your style to suit your relationship with them. Today's writing style is far more relaxed than that of a few years ago, but if you are addressing a new client or contact, for example, a degree of formality is still appropriate, out of politeness. Also, if you are writing to a person who is much older than yourself, again they may well appreciate a more formal approach. However, with someone that you regularly communicate with and know well, a relaxed, friendly style will be well received. You also need to use the right tone for the situation. If you are producing minutes of a meeting going to several people, for example, the tone needs to be informative and concise; concentrate on the key points that occurred. Remember, the aim is always to impart the message in an accessible way.

AIMING FOR GOOD TEXT

Project the right image

Follow an outline

Use language suited to the recipient

Show prior knowledge of the recipient

Provide all the necessary information

KNOWING YOUR SUBJECT

If you are preparing a report, make sure that all the information it contains is well researched. Gather together all the facts and figures by researching in reference books and magazines, looking at CD-ROMs and surfing the Internet. Make sure you have a wealth of data, so that you can eliminate what seems superfluous and keep in the essentials. If you are unsure of the accuracy of some material, check it with two or three other sources to make sure it is correct.

14 Make sure all your information is well researched and substantiated.

When you do research, use as many resources as you can – such as source books or magazines, CD-ROMs, and the internet

Do not rely on your memory for facts – always take notes

 ▲ SORTING THE FACTS
When you have completed your research, sort the information that you have collected into three categories: essential, important, and miscellaneous.

15 Only start writing when you know what you want to say.

ALLOWING FOR RESEARCH TIME

When you are researching, set yourself a time limit as it is easy to spend far longer than you intended. You can easily waste time on the internet, for example, if you are directed to sites that end up being of little use for your needs. Always aim for the most relevant information. Find out in advance from colleagues the best sites to use, or be very specific with the key words you use with your favourite search engine.

PROVIDING THE RIGHT AMOUNT OF INFORMATION

Only give your readers the amount of information that is needed to make a decision or take action. Writers with a traditional science background can write very precisely, while those in the arts tend to have a more fluid style. However, you need to establish a style that is concise in its approach, but also allows for more descriptive paragraphs where a subject needs more elaboration or explanation. If, for example, you try to reduce a report from 15 pages to three, it inevitably means that some vital information will be left out. Cutting out too much information can make the text very bland to read, so that there is not enough descriptive language or clarification of the essential facts. Conversely, sending a long report, written in a convoluted style, will soon lose the interest of the recipients.

16 Make sure that your research is focused.

17 Tailor reports to suit what you know about the recipients.

QUESTIONS TO ASK YOURSELF

Q What does the reader need to know?

Q Why does the reader need this information?

Q What background knowledge does the reader already have?

Q What is the text going to be used for?

Q Who is the intended reader of the text?

Q Are the language and the vocabulary used suitable for the intended reader?

Q Has all the necessary information been included?

PLANNING AND STRUCTURING

When we read something that is written well, it is easy to see its plan and structure. The facts that you are presenting in your text need to be backed up with research material showing how you came to these conclusions, or how you arrived at those statistics. It is also needed to lend substance and credibility to the text that you are presenting. Always make sure that the source of your information is up to date. The financial position of companies or their share price, for example, constantly changes.

Producing good text takes a lot of work, but provided that you have planned well, and put the basic framework into place, you will find that the task is well within your capabilities.

DEFINING YOUR STYLE

If your letter or report is poorly constructed, ambiguously worded, and has grammatical errors, the impression you give of yourself and your skills is not very positive. You need to work on improving your writing style to present an upbeat image.

18 Good writing helps form a relationship between the writer and the reader.

19 Poor writing projects a negative image of both writer and company.

DEVELOPING A CLEAR STYLE

Generally, poor writers have problems developing a clear and concise style. Often their writing technique is old-fashioned and stilted, and the construction of their communications is badly thought out. Poor writers often fall down in their choice of language, using overly formal or technical jargon, or conversely, using language that is too familiar, colloquial, or "slangy". Sentence construction is also a problem, usually because too many words are used when fewer would make the sentence more succinct. Another common problem is using words inappropriately.

▶ **AVOIDING BAD WRITING HABITS**
There are a number of common communication faults, which usually encompass several, if not all, of the stylistic errors described here.

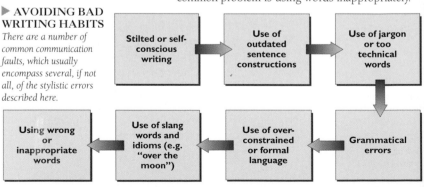

| Stilted or self-conscious writing | → | Use of outdated sentence constructions | → | Use of jargon or too technical words |

| Using wrong or inappropriate words | ← | Use of slang words and idioms (e.g. "over the moon") | ← | Use of over-constrained or formal language | ← | Grammatical errors |

WRITING GOOD TEXT

Poorly written work documents are usually the result of being produced in a hurry without too much thought for the content. As you write, ask yourself:

- Who is this letter written for?
- What is its aim?
- What does the reader need to know?
- Why does the reader need this information?
- What does the reader already know about this subject?

20 Before you start writing, define your target reader and your objectives.

▶ **SHOWING COURTESY AND RESPECT**
This is an example of a poorly written letter that does not even detail the student's full name. The content is confusing, not giving a clear explanation of why the letter is being written.

Using a student number, rather than name, causes offence

Pay the person you are writing to the compliment of addressing them by name

The actual letter does not contain enough information for the reader

The writer signs with initials so there is no contact name

Westfield Independent College
Main Street, Cityville CV2 5SL

Student number 126

Street Name,
Town,
TW4 2BZ,
County   15 July 2002

Dear Sir or Madam,

Please contact the person below at this office as soon as possible in order to sort out a matter relating to you.

Yours faithfully,
LML
Secretary

SOUNDING VERBOSE

Some people write in such a way that it becomes apparent to the reader that they are only interested in telling you what they know. This is conveyed in the text by the addition of obscure or redundant information. Rather than engage with the reader, know-it-all writers try to project their own knowledge, effort, and competence. The end result is writing that is verbose and full of irrelevant information that just serves to irritate or annoy the people who are receiving the communication.

RIGHT

BUYING IN/
CONTRACTING
SERVICES

These procedures conform to legislative requirements.

WRONG

BUYING IN/
CONTRACTING
SERVICES

We have analyzed these items exhaustively and found, at the end of our investigations, that the procedures adopted with regard to the buying in or contracting of services are in line with current legislative requirements.

▲ **GETTING TO THE POINT**
The first text gets straight to the point. The second takes an unnecessarily circuitous route to say the same thing.

CORRECT AND INCORRECT

✔ The aim is to...	✘ The desired end is to...
✔ I can inform you...	✘ We are in the proud position to inform you...
✔ I can let you know that...	✘ We are taking the opportunity of letting you know that...
✔ I am submitting for your approval...	✘ We would like to submit for your approval...
✔ A decision is requested...	✘ We would like to hereby...
✔ Thank you for assisting...	✘ We are truly grateful for...

USING CLICHÉD LANGUAGE

Deferential writers know their place within their organization's hierarchy. They use language that is predictable, sounds false, and verbose, and reflects their preoccupation with hierarchical levels. Such writers also tend to write in well-worn clichés. They may overuse phrases such as, "I will leave this to your better judgment". They have a tendency to use "we" often, which relieves them of the responsibility for their writing, and also indicates a lack of decision-making skills.

SOUNDING INSINCERE

Writers who use jargon extensively are a variation on the know-it-all writer. Jargon-lovers want to convey an image of being up-to-date with the latest business ideas supposedly from top personal development people. Some writers use and repeat sentences and phrases littered with "buzzwords" in the hope that it gives the impression that they are at the cutting edge of what is going on in their particular industry. These unusual, newly-created words and jargon are mostly incomprehensible to a wider audience. This writing style is consciously designed to impress and is quite commonly used where there is competition between individuals within a company. However, to the reader it often sounds insincere and reeks of self-promotion.

21 Resist using buzzwords as they weaken communication.

22 Some words have several meanings or nuances. Try to avoid ambiguity.

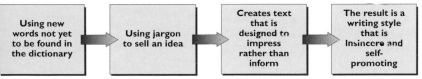

▲ PROMOTING SELF IMPORTANCE
Writing that tries to project an up-to-the-minute feel through the use of new words can make it harder for some readers to understand the writer's meaning.

SPOTTING THE PITFALLS

There are several phrases that can irritate rather than impress the reader, so avoid using any of the following sentences in which you:

- "Attain ceilings".
- "Step up processes".
- "Engage" with others rather than "talk to" or "work with" them.
- Have marketing activities that "impact on" business instead of "have an impact on it".
- "Develop proactive outlooks".
- "Optimize results".
- "Arrive at decisions".
- "Prioritize spaces".
- "Find solutions on a countrywide scale".
- Are "proactive".

WRITING IN A FAKE STYLE

Some people will be impressed with elaborate text, and may even consider it to be creative. However, the more discerning reader will recognize it as fake. Generally speaking, avoid writing embellished texts that bring in certain ethical values and create emphatic views, which can lead to copy full of unsubstantiated statements. Usually this style is adapted to any type of writing, without showing where or how the "supposed" facts originated. So it is a way for the writer who lacks knowledge or ability to hide his personal failings.

The Importance of Thermonuclear Energy

A subject that is talked about very widely nowadays, not only here but also abroad, is the inestimable source of energy provided by thermonuclear power.

Thermonuclear energy is of fundamental importance to modern societies. Without it, humanity would not have experienced the developments that it has made over the last few decades.

This kind of energy, much used in the industrialized world, offers a giant step for mankind towards a peaceful 21st century, with harmony and union between different nations.

In our industrialized and globalized world, the absence of this wonderful source of energy would have led to an impasse with few alternatives for a harmonious relationship between human beings and mother nature – or maybe even survival. We should, therefore, be aware of this gift provided by the genius of man, an everlasting source, which should be used economically or we may run the risk of returning to being simply "king of the beasts."

▲ SOUNDING SELF-IMPORTANT

Writing styles that sustain theauthor's unquestioned views, rather than a sound perspective, are found frequently in business reports.

▶ QUESTIONING VALUES

As a writer, do not lose your credibility by adopting emphatic views to show you lack knowledge and information on a subject.

Embellished texts are a bad writer's way of filling up paper without offering an insight, or balanced view on the subject

23 Be aware of your reader's level of expertise and write with that in mind.

24 Simplicity always impresses more than "trying to impress" text.

SUPPLYING CONFUSING TEXT

Technical language exists to aid communication between those who work in the same field of expertise. When writing in specialized areas avoid causing confusion, which often happens when a writer uses language that is incomprehensible to most, including those in the same discipline.

The letter below does not communicate its message, other than convey the "cleverness" of the author. Sentences are convoluted, and aim to show off the writer's education and knowledge of Latin. The author confuses the reader and does not say what he means, which is that he disagrees with a decision made by the people to whom he is writing.

◀ **CONVEYING INFORMATION**

This quirky style does not communicate very much. The writer is more interested in demonstrating his or her own knowledge and education than in objectively conveying ideas.

Distinguished Sirs,

Although keen to express my warmest felicitations and acknowledge the deep honour your request bestows upon me, I feel that the reasoning behind your policy decision, which is enough to make wise men quick to cry out like the furies of ancient times, angers me beyond belief.

Your decision occasions the *onus probandi* to lie firmly on my shoulders, yet in these parlous times, those beings of limited ability are inseparable from those with superior knowledge, many of the latter residing so near to Mt. Olympus as to be unreachable.

For these reasons I regret that I am forced into declining your most felicitous invitation.

Your most honoured servant,

Evidence that the writer is trying to show off a knowledge of Latin in the text

This text may only irritate the reader

UNDERSTANDING THE BASICS

Once you know the basic techniques, you have the tools to write well. It is worthwhile spending time building a wide vocabulary and developing a flowing style with good sentence construction.

TAKING THE FIRST STEPS

Writing in a good style comes from three main activities: reading, writing, and rewriting. Reading provides you with the background vocabulary for writing; writing itself develops your style; rewriting helps refine your technique.

25 Reading different materials helps you write creatively.

26 As you gain more knowledge, your writing style will benefit.

READING WIDELY

When you read extensively you can discover useful information, develop your vocabulary, and learn about different writing styles. Reading newspapers, magazines, and a variety of books helps you gain as much information as possible. Absorbing different writing styles will enrich your own vocabulary, show you how different people write, and deepen your knowledge of many subject areas. By becoming well-read, you will feel more confident in how you write, and be better able to relate information and express your opinions in an informed manner.

IMPROVING YOUR WRITING

Writing should not be seen as a chore. With advance planning and careful thought, letters, memos, reports, and proposals can be produced to a high standard. Before starting, think about what you are trying to achieve: letters need to be polite because they represent the good image of the company, reports summarise many hours of research, interviews, and data collection, while proposals show the final presentation of a developing idea. Draft out the information you wish to convey, leave it for a while, then read it aloud to yourself to see how it sounds. Look for any awkward phrasing, bad sentence construction, or colloquialisms that may be inappropriate.

27 Always look critically at everything you write.

28 Find out how other professionals write in your subject area.

Manager and employee discuss informally how the department report should look

ACCEPTING ADVICE

When writing, think carefully about your attitude to your written work. Remember that whenever you write something, someone else may want to change it. If you show a draft report to your boss, for example, do not think it is a reflection on your abilities or intelligence if he or she suggests making several changes or additions. Instead, try to look at the comments in a constructive way, seeing how they are improving or enhancing the structure or content of your text. Often people who have more distance can give a better judgment and more objective assessment of what you have written.

◀ TAKING ON CRITICISM
After you have written something, be prepared to discuss it frankly and receive comments or changes from your manager or an office colleague.

23

COMPOSING GOOD SENTENCES

The sentence is the central part of any piece of writing, and needs to contain a subject, verb, and an object. Think about the correct vocabulary for the subject you are writing about, and beware of making grammatical mistakes.

29 Structure sentences well, so that the reader does not lose interest.

30 Avoid using empty phrases or including any superfluous information which sounds imprecise.

WRITING CONCISELY

When writing you will often find that using one word is more effective than two or three together. Always write concisely, concentrating on the essential information you want to impart. Flowery or superfluous language will only irritate the reader or detract from the main points you are trying to make. The letter, report, or other document that you are sending will then take less time to read, which the reader will appreciate.

CONSTRUCTING CONCISE SENTENCES

AVOID	USE
During the year 2002	In 2002
Fines were applied in line with the relevant regulations	The regulatory fines were applied
We wish to make the most of this opportunity to inform you ...	We would like to tell you ...
We would like to request that you proceed to collect the debts ...	Please collect the debts now ...

USING THE RIGHT WORD

Finding the right word for what you want to convey needs a wide vocabulary and an awareness of the possible connotations in language. If in doubt check your dictionary. Here are a few pitfalls from using the wrong choice of words:

- Words that have several meanings just make the reader laugh. For example, "The cook gently laid the eggs in the fridge." Chickens lay eggs, but people "place" eggs in the fridge.
- When words are used out of context it can cause confusion. For example, "The fireman committed an act of bravery." People commit robberies, but "perform" acts of bravery.
- Words that are not used correctly can cause confusion. For example, "The accusations will be received by Procon." Accusations in this context are "heard", not received.
- Avoid unintentional puns. For example, "Dracula knew there was a lot at stake over what happened next."

QUESTIONS TO ASK YOURSELF

Q Is the word used known to everyone, or is it a strictly technical term?

Q Even though it is in the dictionary, is this word commonly used?

Q Is the chosen word the best one to use in this particular context?

Q Does the word help inform the reader, or are you using it to show off your vocabulary?

Q Are the foreign terms used appropriate in the context, and will they be readily understood by the reader?

31 Check the meaning of words and your vocabulary will improve.

32 Avoid contextual mistakes or people will laugh at you, not with you.

AVOIDING REPETITION

Try not to write in a repetitious way or use tautology. As well as padding out the text unnecessarily, these stylistic mistakes will only make the reader laugh. Look at the following examples (redundant words are in heavy type):

- It is necessary to start **the initialization** of the project.
- We want to keep the **same** payment conditions.
- The **highly** unique award was given to an employee in accounts.
- It was **an unexpected** surprise to receive an invitation to the opening of the **new** shop.
- Full-time dedication to the project is expected **at all times**.

USING DIFFERENT VOICES

There are different kinds of language that you can use in day-to-day business. These include: the "active voice", which can make your communications more effective, and the "passive voice", if you want to sound polite or avoid sounding aggressive.

33 Writing in the passive voice generates a less aggressive approach.

34 Short sentences are useful for conveying certain information.

BEING ACTIVE

Sentences in the active voice are shorter and livelier. In this type of sentence, the subject does something, for example, "The department requests the information". With sentences in the passive tense something happens to the subject, for example, "Information was requested by the department". However, using the passive voice to much can make text seem flabby and flat. When referring to your company, or to those who work for it, the active voice conveys real assertiveness and a direct style.

CORRECT AND INCORRECT

✔ Zedcom is building new laboratories.

✔ Zedcom is launching three new promotions in April.

✔ Zedcom is developing a social assistance programme for those on a low income.

✘ New laboratories are being built by Zedcom.

✘ Three new promotions are being launched by Zedcom in April.

✘ Social assistance programmes are being developed by Zedcom for those on a low income.

35 The active voice is best if you want to be assertive or inspirational.

BEING DIPLOMATIC

Athough the active voice is normally recommended for most communications, there are times when a more diplomatic, passive style is preferred, so that the negative impact of certain information is reduced. There are occasions when you may need to deal with an ongoing conflict, for example, turn down an exployee for promotion, point out mistakes, or reprimand a member of staff, and a friendly but firm writing style is preferred. The secret is knowing how to pass on the necessary information in a way that will not cause upset between employees or other departments in the company. Using the passive voice on these occasions can make the information you are sending seem less abrupt or aggressive, softening the impact of what you are obliged to say.

36 Saying "no" to someone sounds better in the passive voice.

37 To adopt a diplomatic writing style, imagine the person is standing in front of you.

EMPLOYING THE PASSIVE VOICE

ABRUPT TONE	LESS AGGRESSIVE TONE
The clinic cannot tell you your result because you have not paid last month's bill.	Your result cannot be provided as there is a payment outstanding.
This is the estimate for the repairs to the window that your son broke last Thursday.	Here is the estimate for the repairs to the window that was broken last Thursday.
We are going to dismiss three workers tomorrow.	Three workers are going to be dismissed tomorrow.
The auditor handling the inspection noticed fraudulent activity in the company accounts.	Fraudulent activity has been noted in the company accounts by the auditor.

CHOOSING WORDS FOR EMPHASIS

When you are writing to clients or colleagues, you need to make it clear what you want them to do. Indicate whether the task is essential or if there is some choice involved. The verbs "may/can", "must", and "should" are recognized as being the most suitable for expressing what you require of the person to whom you are writing.

38 When giving instructions, always avoid ambiguous terms.

▼ **IN PRACTICE**
The examples below show how you can express your requirements with the right emphasis.

KNOW WHEN TO USE "MUST", "MAY/CAN", AND "SHOULD"

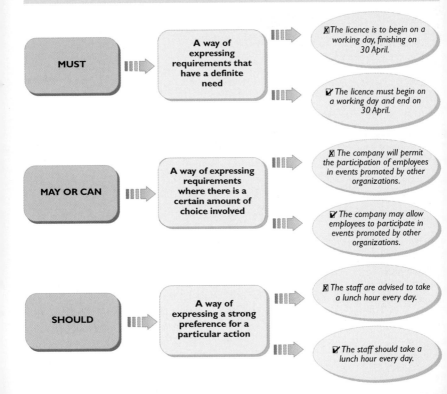

MUST ▶ A way of expressing requirements that have a definite need

▶ ☒ The licence is to begin on a working day, finishing on 30 April.

▶ ☑ The licence must begin on a working day and end on 30 April.

MAY OR CAN ▶ A way of expressing requirements where there is a certain amount of choice involved

▶ ☒ The company will permit the participation of employees in events promoted by other organizations.

▶ ☑ The company may allow employees to participate in events promoted by other organizations.

SHOULD ▶ A way of expressing a strong preference for a particular action

▶ ☒ The staff are advised to take a lunch hour every day.

▶ ☑ The staff should take a lunch hour every day.

USING PLAIN ENGLISH

Many people overcomplicate their writing in the belief that the reader will be impressed by unusual words or complex language. However, plain language is easier to follow and will keep the reader's interest. Remember that you are writing to communicate, so a good rule is to try to write as you speak. Aim to avoid overly formal language or officialese. Archaic language and very complex sentences are confusing and mostly redundant. Use concise phrases that get straight to the point.

 39 Be accurate. Use nouns rather than several pronouns.

AVOIDING AMBIGUITY

AMBIGUOUS SENTENCE	SPECIFIC SENTENCE
Before leaving, check that the lift has stopped at the right floor.	Before leaving the lift, check that it has stopped at the right floor.
Attention, passengers for Flight 168! We would like to inform you that when boarding is announced, it will be through gate nine.	Attention, passengers! Boarding for Flight 168 will be through gate nine. Listen for the announcement.
During the assault, the thieves used knives and two guns. They were later found in the river.	During the assault, the thieves used knives and two guns. The weapons were later found in the river.
There were a lot of visitors to the Olympic Games. To put them up, the hotel network had to be expanded.	To accommodate the high number of visitors to the Olympic Games, the hotel network had to be expanded.
The film contains sex, bad language, and violence, which is unsuitable for children.	The film contains sex, bad language, and violence. It is unsuitable for children.

KNOWING THE RULES

A sound knowledge of grammar will lend credibility to your writing, although it will not necessarily improve your style. Do not allow yourself to become preoccupied with different points of grammar, as it is important to maintain your creative flow.

40 Use a dictionary and check your grammar when rewriting.

41 Write freely at first, but reread and correct later.

WRITING FREELY

You should not worry too much about the grammar you are using when you are in the act of writing. If you hesitate for too long over the right tense to use, where to put apostrophes, or whether it is a single or plural noun you will never write anything. Write a first draft of what you want to say and then appraise it later, correcting any obvious mistakes that you have made.

PROJECTING AN IMAGE

If you do send out communications that contain grammatical errors, it can compromise not only the quality of the information being presented, but it will also reflect on your professional image. Spelling mistakes can occur because of laziness, careless writing, or simply lack of knowledge. If you know that you have a problem with spelling or sentence construction, check what you have written carefully. Also consider getting a colleague, who you think has a good grasp of grammar, to look over what you have done and make useful comments.

Nick Eccles
Lawyer

Foster and Harding Co. Ltd.,
Civil, Crimnal, and Family Law
11 Street Square, Ardean, Perthshire
Telephone: 02131 333 5455

▲ **CREATING A GOOD IMPRESSION**
Making a spelling error on your business card does not promote a positive or professional image to potential clients.

MAKING USE OF OTHER RESOURCES

When you are writing, make use of all the information resources available on the Internet. You can use different search engines to source directories or other research material for the subject on which you are writing. Many successful writers create their own thesaurus of different words to use, and you may find this works for you. This can be particularly useful if you have to write or report regularly on the same subject. You can add in interesting quotations, extracts, or maybe cartoons, if these are appropriate.

USING A DICTIONARY REGULARLY

If you need to use a dictionary regularly to check your spelling or to look up the actual meaning of a word, you should not feel embarrassed. In fact, it reflects well on you as it shows that you are concerned about the standard of your writing and want to present it to the people concerned in the best possible way.

42 Knowing basic grammar rules is just the start of writing well.

43 Correct spelling is essential for credible communications.

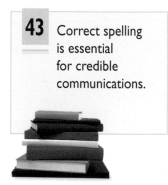

44 Explore the dictionary widely to improve your vocabulary.

RECOMMENDED REFERENCE BOOKS

When you write regularly, it is a good idea to have several reference books to hand to check your content. Generally, an extensive dictionary and a book on grammar usage are the most useful. Look in bookshops and libraries for the best ones available, and ask which ones are preferred by editors and writers. If you are writing about specific subjects, you might also think about getting some encyclopedias and other reference guides that will help you find other information.

USING CORRECT GRAMMAR

Clear and grammatical writing is mainly a matter of common sense. If you can read and understand this book, then you are already familiar with basic grammar and how it helps to get your message across clearly and concisely. Start by forgetting about grammar. Just relax and write as if you were talking to another person and trying to explain something. You can then rewrite your text and correct the spelling and syntax as you edit. Syntax just means the grammatical structure of the sentence that gives it precision and meaning.

45 Keep your use of foreign words and phrases to a minimum.

46 Cut down on slang, jargon, buzzwords, and clichés.

PARTS OF SPEECH

- ADJECTIVES are words that describe a noun or a pronoun.
- ADVERBS are words or phrases qualifying verbs, adjectives, sentences or clauses.
- NOUNS name or identify a thing or a person.
- PREPOSITIONS show the relation of one word to another, e.g. position, direction, and time.
- PRONOUNS take the place of a noun or a word group. There are five types: personal (I, you, he, we), relative (that, what, which, whose), interrogative (who, which, what), demonstrative (that, this, those), indefinite (both, each, many, one, other).
- VERBS express action or a state of being.

IMPROVING YOUR TEXT

It is a good idea to read what you have written out loud afterwards. Good writing has a rhythm just like music. You will know if your style is good if it flows together and does not sound awkward. If any of part of your text sounds unintelligible, unnecessarily formal, pretentious, or is difficult to read without catching your breath (which means that your sentences are too long!), you will need to change it. Try breaking up the longer sentences into two or three shorter ones, each conveying a key point. To help you brush up on your basic grammar and give yourself confidence, look at the tips on grammar and usage in the tables opposite. Read as much good writing as you can from books, newspapers, magazines, and published reports. The more you read, the more you will subconsciously learn about good grammar, vocabulary, and style. Remember, English is a living, breathing language, so you are bound to use many everyday words to get your message across.

AVOIDING TYPICAL ERRORS

COMMON ERRORS	CORRECTED ERRORS
ADJECTIVES	
... the **principle** reason for...	... the **principal** reason for ...
... the recently **floating** company...	... the recently **floated** company ...
Managers' incompetence means that...	**Managerial** incompetence means that ...
SUPERLATIVES	
His results were **worst** than hers.	His results were **worse** than hers.
My leg hurts **bad.**	My leg hurts **badly.**
... a **sound,** written constitution. ..	... a **soundly** written constitution ...
CAPITALIZATION	
If you look in the **Preface** ...	If you look in the **preface** ...
The **Queen** of England ...	The **queen** of England ...
The **chairman of the board** announced ...	The **Chairman of the Board** announced ...
CONJUNCTIONS	
The next picture **that** is shown here ...	The next picture, **which** is shown here ...
Neither the book **or** the pen were found.	Neither the book **nor** the pen were found.
Insomnia is **because** you cannot sleep.	Insomnia is **when** you cannot sleep.
NOUNS	
He was treated by a **councillor.**	He was treated by a **counsellor.**
... the **smile** on the **face** of the staff ...	... the **smiles** on the **faces** of the staff ...
The **seller** was very helpful.	The **salesperson** was very helpful.
PREPOSITIONS	
My term of office is **for** six months.	My term of office is six months.
...my interest and concern for the staff...	... my interest **in** and concern for the staff ...
... diplomacy **among** EU members ...	... diplomacy **between** EU members ...
PRONOUNS	
I do not know **whom** is stealing from **who.**	I do not know **who** is stealing from **whom.**
I solved the problem **with** my PC.	I solved the problem **on** my PC.
Between you and **I,** the office is a mess!	Between you and **me,** the office is a mess!
PUNCTUATION	
So to conclude; **We** must work harder!	So to conclude: **we** must work harder!
For more details see Chapter 10.	For more details, see Chapter 10.
The firm held **it's** AGM on ...	The firm held **its** AGM on ...
VERBS	
... bad weather **effected** deliveries ...	... bad weather **affected** deliveries ...
... the manager and his staff **is** coming ...	... the manager and his staff **are** coming ...
I looked to see if he **were** there ...	I looked to see if he **was** there ...

PRESENTING YOUR WORK

Generally, anything that is produced without effort must be read with great effort. It's not enough to simply write well. Knowing a little about fonts, colours, and layout can help you produce printed materials that are more interesting and attractive for the reader.

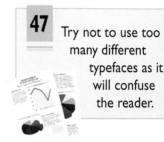

47 Try not to use too many different typefaces as it will confuse the reader.

USING FONTS TO MAKE AN IMPACT

FONTS	EXAMPLES
SERIF FONTS Serif lines are little lines that finish off strokes of individual letters and lead the eye across the line. These fonts are usually used in the body of a text.	This report must be sent out to all our customers as soon as possible.
FONTS WITHOUT SERIFS (SANS SERIFS) These are modern-looking fonts. Using uppercase and bold, a title with impact can be created. They are often used in headings, margins, posters, and so on.	**HOW TO WRITE CLEARLY**
SUBHEADS WITHOUT SERIFS Subheads within a text that use a font without a serif are used to provide a distinctive contrast.	**Technical-Scientific Report** A document that formally details the results or developments obtained through in-depth investigations, or that describes the current thinking on a technical or scientific question.

CHOOSING THE RIGHT FONT

Do you want to write a text that grabs the reader's attention or one that is elegant and serious? You can create the impression you want by choosing an appropriate type style, or font. All modern word-processing packages are set up so that you can produce texts that are visually attractive, using a wide choice of different fonts. Remember to keep it simple. In general, the best ideas are those that make the reader stop and think for a second, with a little envy, "Why didn't I think of that?"

48 Write the text first, then think about how you want it to look.

FONTS

SCRIPT FONTS
These fonts produce letters that look handwritten but are old-fashioned. They are ideal for personalized texts such as letterheads and invitations. If used as an opening to a business proposal, they can lend a touch of elegance.

UNUSUAL FONTS
You can vary the look of your text by using unusual fonts that will grab the reader's attention. But be careful: overuse of this method may make the text appear less serious. When sending faxes, avoid elaborate fonts and background colours.

THINK ABOUT THE SIZE OF THE FONTS YOU USE
Between 10 and 12 points is usual, although this varies for headers, posters, and so on.

EXAMPLES

These fonts produce letters that look handwritten. They are ideal for personalized texts such as letterheads and invitations.

PERSPECTIVES FOR UNDERSTANDING ORGANIZATIONS

8 points
10 points
12 points
14 points

49 Choose colours that suit the content of your text and your reader.

50 Use colours subtly so that you do not turn your text into a gaudy, showy document.

ADDING IMAGES

Using photos, drawings, and figures adds life to a text and can make it easier to understand. However, if you use too many, you will do the opposite and confuse and distract the reader. If you are using colour, apply it consistently. Applying different colours to headings within a single text is more appropriate for text aimed at children than adults.

WRONG

RIGHT

DISTRACTING THE READER ▶

Reproduce titles and figures in their simplest font. If you italicize them, take them out of focus, or place them over text, you will destroy them. Make sure that whatever image or figure you use attracts the reader's attention to the text, not away from it.

SPACING AND TYPE

When leaflets or reports have a long heading, make the text bold to stand out, and also try increasing the spacing between words as this can make it easier to read. The body text should be in a clear, easy-to-read type, centred under the heading to give it more prominence.

THE TOURIST ENTERTAINMENT ROUTE

Expanded heading in a bold type

A route of bars, beaches, discotheques, and restaurants to help you enjoy yourself in ten capitals.

Clear typeface with copy centred under heading

51 Visual aids help grab the reader's attention.

ILLUSTRATING YOUR TEXT

Charts and tables are of considerable value when explaining certain concepts, statistics, or demonstrating facts. Often, large amounts of plain text are not as good as illustrated text because the reader becomes confused or bored when they are inundated with so much solid information. Charts and tables allow the reader to understand the whole concept being discussed, and show visual examples of different points.

▼ IMPORTING CHARTS
There are a number of pre-programmed charts available on most computers. The most common are pie and bar charts.

Columns or bars show the percentage of respondents

Each "portion" of the pie represents a percentage

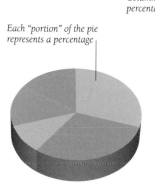

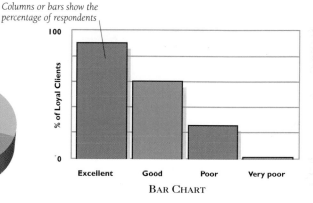

PIE CHART

BAR CHART

MAKING USE OF LABELS

Get the most out of any images you have included by adding labels or captions that add emphasis to what is being shown visually. Write these descriptions carefully so that they add to the visual impact of the illustration. Bear in mind that you are trying to arouse the reader's interest in the topic, so write points that are punchy, and that add interesting facts.

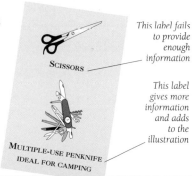

This label fails to provide enough information

SCISSORS

This label gives more information and adds to the illustration

MULTIPLE-USE PENKNIFE IDEAL FOR CAMPING

37

WRITING POSITIVELY

Producing text that emphasizes the positive aspects of the information you are generating will make a stronger impression on your recipients. Also, be careful to write in a way that avoids any form of discrimination.

52 Good writers always present the positives, rather than the negatives.

53 Always ensure that you write in a non-discriminatory way.

BEING SUBTLE

A text which has a positive rather than negative emphasis will always be better received. Instead of writing, "Do not forget", write, "Remember". Rather than writing, "The container should not be boarded with the cooling equipment", write, "The container should be boarded without the cooling equipment".

As well as being negative, this communication confuses the reader

TAKING THE RIGHT ▶ APPROACH

The emphasis of this letter is quite negative, reflecting badly on the institute. The fact that a grant has been awarded, albeit for the following year, is only detailed in the last paragraph. By saying initially: "Your request for a grant has received approval...", the reader will feel positive, despite discovering later on in the letter that the date of approval is in fact later than originally requested.

CETED/PG
Street Name
Big City

Today's date

Ms. J Hartley
Street Name
Big City

Dear Ms. Hartley,

Re: Your application for an overseas study grant

Unfortunately, following a decision made by this foundation, all grant requests for overseas study not received by the date stated have been rejected. This decision relates to recent changes in government grants to this institution.

However, the budget for next year has been set, and your grant will be awarded early next year.

Yours sincerely,

Steven Milner

AVOIDING DISCRIMINATION

Be careful about adopting a discriminatory style when writing as it can:

- Render people invisible.
- Highlight physical or intellectual limitations rather than other positive personal characteristics.
- Describe people in stereotypical terms.
- Be insensitive to people's social position and needs, or be too focused on those aspects.
- Use terms that are considered negative, or are thought to be derogatory to certain groups of people.

CORRECT AND INCORRECT

✔ Black	✘ Coloured	
✔ Low-income families	✘ Poor families	
✔ Special needs	✘ Retarded	
✔ Sensory impaired	✘ Deaf or blind	
✔ Partner	✘ Boyfriend/girlfriend	

Key

❶ *By not detailing who was involved, the majority of employees are discriminated against in this chairman's memo, even though they are not involved and probably should not be receiving it.*

❷ *This implies that Ms. Smith's disability makes her less competent than her able-bodied colleagues, even though she has broken the sales record.*

❸ *This is implicit discrimination, since it brings attention to Mr Brown's lack of qualifications. The wording makes an unnecessary comparison with those associates who have degrees.*

❹ *It is the wife's position as the co-ordinator that is relevant, not her husband's job, or her beauty.*

❺ *Mentioning skin colour is irrelevant and can be construed by many as discriminatory or racist.*

❶ We have been informed that two employees have been misappropriating company office materials.

❷ Our winner is Ms. Smith, who despite being a wheelchair user, managed to break the sales record in August. Well done, Ms Smith!

❸ We would like to congratulate Mr. Brown, who, despite not having a university degree, has been promoted to a managerial position.

❹ The Chief Engineer's beautiful wife was asked to speak in her role as co-ordinator of the SAC.

❺ Five people, one of them black, have been recruited to the department.

◀ **USING DISCRIMINATORY LANGUAGE**
These examples show five main types of language use which should be avoided at all costs.

COMMUNICATING WITH THE READER

When there is a tight deadline, the temptation is to write hurriedly, paying little attention to the way you express yourself. But this can often send a confusing or wrong message to the reader, so take time to write well and communicate clearly.

54 Your writing style should not upset the reader or lose their attention.

55 Have a final read of your text before you send it.

COMMUNICATING WELL

If a company is to have a friendly working environment, the communication channels, both spoken and written, between colleagues need to be amiable and efficient. When tense situations arise, this informal atmosphere can help when trying to resolve major problems or deadlocks. The same principles can be applied to existing clients and suppliers.

CASE STUDY

It was Andrea's birthday and she received a beautiful bouquet of flowers from her boss. The next day, she sent him a thank-you card, worded as follows:

Dear Robert,
Many thanks for my birthday flowers. I was really surprised at your kindness – it made me very happy.
Andrea

Andrea was a typical writer in a hurry and did not re-read what she had written. The text had an underlining meaning that Robert is normally rude and offensive, which is why she was surprised. If she had opted for "I was delighted" or "Your kindness was so thoughtful", she would have maintained the cordiality that needs to exist in all day-to-day situations.

◀ **WRITING IN HASTE**
In this example, Andrea did not take enough care when writing to thank her boss for the flowers. Andrea should have reread the text, noticed the unpleasant undertone, and then changed the style of the note so that it expressed her feelings more sincerely.

FINDING THE RIGHT TONE

In spoken language, what we say can often be softened and modified. You can say that you were misunderstood, that you did not say something, or that you were misheard. But everything we write down can sound stark and formal. Because of this, follow these simple rules:

● Avoid terse or impersonal phrases, as your reader will take offence.

● Present bad news in an objective manner. There is always a better way to say something.

● Do not think you are infallible; apologizing can be a good way forward in business.

LETTER OF COMPLAINT

INDIFFERENCE TO THE CUSTOMER

Dear PGF,

I am writing to complain about the Internet service I am receiving in the Liverpool area. I often cannot get online because of server disruption, and when I call the customer helpline for an explanation it is always engaged.

I am totally frustrated and am considering changing providers. Can [you sugge]st any positive changes you [are makin]g to improve the service and [your c]ustom?

Yours sincerely,

Jane Smith

Dear Ms. Smith,

We have many customers using our Internet service and inevitably some problems are experienced with our server from time to time. There has been no record of increased problems in your area, and other customers are able to access our helpline easily.

However, we have made a note of your complaint.

Yours sincerely,

J. Henry

PGF Customer Service

CONCERN FOR THE CUSTOMER

Dear Ms. Smith,

I am sorry for all the disruption you have been experiencing with our server. We aim to give the best service to our customers, and have started work on improving access and making the server more reliable.

We will contact you again in a few days, explaining the improvements we are making to our present system.

I do apologize once again.

Yours sincerely,

J. Henry

PGF Customer Service Department

Dear Mr. McManus,

Re: Account no: 12767899

I am sorry we cannot grant your request for a loan this month, but it will be reviewed in a few weeks' time.

I regret this inconvenience, but I am sure we will be able to accommodate your needs shortly.

Yours sincerely

D. O'Faolain

Bank Manager

▲ BEING PLEASANT

In this letter the loan has been refused, but only temporarily. In the tone of the letter the bank manager treats his client in a considerate manner.

▲ BEING UNHELPFUL

The tone of the first letter indicates that the Internet company is not interested in their customer's problem and does not offer any useful solutions. The second letter is more positive and addresses the problem immediately, offering to give further information on how they will improve their system.

STRUCTURING YOUR WRITING

Having learned the skills and techniques for writing readable text, you need to understand how to structure your work, and how to establish an efficient way of working.

ESTABLISHING PROCEDURES

There is no single way of getting your message across. Everyone has an individual method. However, there are a number of steps in the writing process through which every text needs to pass.

56 Ensure your text flows from section to section.

57 Think of your topic, then plan how to get the idea across.

58 Compose your text as a musician might write a piece of music.

PLANNING YOUR WORK

It is vital that your text makes sense from start to finish. So, before you begin to write, plan exactly how you are going to convey the various aspects of the topic in a straightforward way. Whether your text is a one-page memorandum or an extensive report, you will need a beginning, a middle, and an end. All your paragraphs need to flow from one to the other to create a whole. After an introductory paragraph, the second paragraph should flow onto the next, and so on, until a logical and effective conclusion is reached.

59 Connecting all of its parts logically will ensure your text makes sense.

ORGANIZING THE TEXT

For the text to work well, it must include:

● An introduction. This should outline the subject and clarify the aim of the text.

● Development. This longer section should set out new information and discuss, prove, compare, contradict, and justify the source of the information presented.

● Conclusion. This section will bring together and summarize the relevant points, reaffirming new information, and should also include the author's personal conclusions.

CONDUCTING RESEARCH

You must have in-depth knowledge of the subject you are going to write about. You will need to have relevant information to hand. To do this, gather together and organize your data. This task has been made easier by the Internet, which can make massive amounts of knowledge and information accessible to all. Once you have finished your research, organize your results either as computer files or as documents in a filing cabinet.

Create computer files and make back-up copies of the most important documents

File your research documents for instant access

STORING ▶ INFORMATION
Set up a suitable filing system and ensure that it is efficient. The definitive test is always being able to find what you want quickly.

PRODUCING AN OUTLINE

Always prepare an outline of your text by listing all the ideas and information that you feel will be relevant to the document you are writing. At this stage, do not worry about the order in which you jot down your ideas. Just write everything down that comes into your head. When you have finished the list, read what you have written with a more critical eye and begin to eliminate irrelevant ideas, details, and questions. Use this method to get rid of everything that will be superfluous to the reader. Finally, you need to combine the ideas and information that you have decided to keep, listing them in order, from greatest to least importance. This is your outline.

60 With an outline by your side, you will not get lost.

61 Separate what the reader needs to know from what is merely of interest.

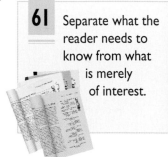

62 All new information needs to be backed up with evidence.

QUESTIONS TO ASK YOURSELF

Q Do I have enough background knowledge to deal with the subject in question?

Q Have I included all the relevant facts and information?

Q Have I recorded the sources of my information?

Q Have I given enough thought to the organization of the text?

Q Have I got my message over efficiently and effectively?

STARTING TO WRITE

Using your outline, write freely and do not be afraid to put down any thoughts, however imperfectly expressed. Do not necessarily start at the beginning. Begin by developing the ideas that you feel are easiest to deal with. You should not lose your way, because the outline will list all the ideas that you should cover in your text. It will take time to work out the paragraph structure. Once you have decided the subject for each paragraph, order them logically to follow the chosen structure and achieve a flowing text. Do not be tempted to read and rewrite the text as soon as you have finished your main points. Leave it alone for a short time. Then you will have the necessary critical distance to be able to revise what you have written more effectively and efficiently.

**Read the text
right through**

Make the first corrections

**Ask somebody else
to read your text**

**Make any corrections that
you feel are necessary**

**Leave the text to
"rest" for a while**

Do a final reading

REVISING AND REWRITING

After a careful read-through, rewrite your text where necessary. Check to see whether or not the information is organized in the clearest way possible and also whether your use of vocabulary is appropriate. Then, make the required corrections, consulting dictionaries, a thesaurus, and grammar reference books. Look at, and revise the layout of all the information, including illustrations if they are being included. Once again, cut out anything that is not useful or which is not wholly relevant, so that what is left conveys your message perfectly and precisely. Then ask a colleague's opinion, add in any valid comments, and leave the text to "rest" for a while. Finally, have one last read-through before you send it out to colleagues or clients.

▼ SHOWING YOUR TEXT TO A COLLEAGUE
Accepting suggestions for changes made by colleagues is halfway to producing a good result. Be objective and open to new ideas and criticisms.

ASKING FOR OPINIONS

Hearing the opinions of others on your text will help you to detect any of your faults. Often, what appears to be totally clear to you will be confusing for your reader, who may feel that the paragraphs are not clearly connected, or that the text does not make sense. It is difficult to spot such problems on your own.

Colleagues point out any errors or problems they feel exist directly on screen.

USING THE INVERTED PYRAMID

The inverted pyramid system provides a logical structure for writing text. It enables you to write down information in an ordered sequence, according to what is most important. This structure is the one most frequently used by business writers.

63 The inverted pyramid format is ideal for executive summaries.

64 Put essential detail first, supporting data next, and additional data last.

APPLYING THE TECHNIQUE

The pyramid structure is ideal for writing general business communications and announcements, for example company results, invitations to participate in events, and employment notices. It is also ideal for producing executive summaries and other business documents that require you to provide condensed information in a report format that is understandable to everyone. Journalists also use this technique for writing news stories and reports.

Main information

Examples, back-up information, arguments that support essential information

Additional information

65 Do not confuse your reader with irrelevant details.

◀ **PROVIDING A STRUCTURE**
These are the three essential elements that comprise the structure of the pyramid and make for clearer, more concise writing.

66 Information should be competently, professionally, and politely presented.

67 Employment offers may be set out using the inverted pyramid structure.

WRITING BUSINESS MEMOS

This structure is ideal for in-house communications and memos. In the example below, Mr Prest receives a briefing from the Human Resources Department at InfoPower about his staff's standard working day. He finds the content difficult and confusing to read. The HR department is not practised at writing memos – and it shows. Had they used the pyramid structure, their memo would have been much shorter and clearer.

▼ **BEING ORGANIZED**
The memo on the left does not deliver its message because it is unclear, badly organized, and was not checked before it was sent out. The reader is left uncertain about what action to take. The memo below is clearer and more direct.

Support information

Essential information

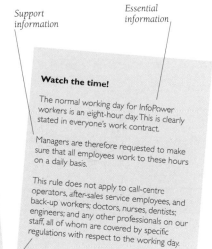

HUMAN RESOURCES DEPARTMENT

COMMUNICATION/WORKING DAY

As set out in Personnel Regulations, the working day at InfoPower is eight hours a day for all employees, apart from those in certain positions that have their own specific regulations (i.e., call-centre operators, after-sales service, and back-up staff) or when legal requirements state otherwise, such as those working as: doctors, dentists, engineers, work safety professionals, nurses, doctors, computer operators, and data-entry operators.
We therefore wish to alert those in management positions that basic company rulings must be adhered to on the standard working day and that no modifications may be made to the conditions set out in individual works contracts.

Watch the time!

The normal working day for InfoPower workers is an eight-hour day. This is clearly stated in everyone's work contract.

Managers are therefore requested to make sure that all employees work to these hours on a daily basis.

This rule does not apply to call-centre operators, after-sales service employees, and back-up workers; doctors, nurses, dentists; engineers; and any other professionals on our staff, all of whom are covered by specific regulations with respect to the working day.

INCORRECT EXAMPLE

Additional information

USING THE PYRAMID STRUCTURE

WRITING BUSINESS REPORTS

There are three stages to writing a report. First, outline what your report will cover. Next, provide the details to back up your case. Finally, finish with a summary of the contents, or a list of conclusions based on the facts presented.

68 The essence of report writing is to make the facts clear and succinct.

COMMUNICATING FACTS

Report writing can cover many forms of communication. It is widely used in business for keeping managers and staff informed of developments in other departments, or between company and client. The report format is also used for making presentations.

Introduce subject areas

Elaborate on subject areas in more detail, breaking them down under subject headings

Provide a summary or conclusion

69 Your report should follow the outline of the introduction.

70 Reports should inform, clarify, and draw a conclusion.

◀ **STRUCTURING THE REPORT**
The report structure enables the writer to stick to the relevant points and provide a clear summary. Readers should not be in any doubt about the goals and suggested outcome detailed in the report.

Report title should clearly outline content

Report on Internet Requirements for Production Department

There is a requirement for quicker Internet access within the Production Department. Access to research sources is vital for the smooth running of the department. We believe that we can provide an efficient service within the allocated budget.

Outline the problem clearly

We propose to do this in the following stages:

● Install ISDN lines for all seven staff.

● Upgrade seven PCs purchased three years ago to bring them in line with current working needs.

● Use redundant Production Department PCs in the stock-room, where computer speed is less important.

● An estimated 20% of the cost will be saved.

Use bullet points, numbers, or other graphic devices to emphasize each point

71 Do not pass on unsubstantiated facts. Always make it clear if you are making a personal judgment, rather than relating facts.

▲ UTILIZING THE REPORT STRUCTURE

Good report writing makes the facts clear, without any unnecessary padding. Use headings to highlight a change in subject and sub-headings for related themes. Make sure your page layout is clear and easy to follow.

USING QUESTIONS AND ANSWERS

You can use the question-and-answer format to provide information in a document by answering a number of questions that are frequently asked. When properly implemented, this style is extremely instructive and informative.

72 Anticipate the most common problems the reader might have.

73 Do not confuse by asking multiple questions. Just ask one at a time.

CONVEYING INFORMATION

The question-and-answer structure is very useful when you need to inform a varied public audience about something, or when you have a lot of information to convey, for example, to explain how to use a piece of equipment, fill in a form, or follow a set of instructions. By using this format, the reader is able to select the information they want, as you will have anticipated the most likely questions they may have when attempting to carry out your instructions.

ESTABLISHING THE QUESTIONS

● Have a brainstorming session with colleagues so that you can try and list all the possible queries that a reader might have.
● Only select the most common problems or queries. If you mention all the possible areas of difficulty in your text, you may create more problems than most people would have.
● Write down the questions in the most colloquial manner possible. This will make the text feel more like a "conversation".
● Give answers that directly address the question so that the reader will be able to act on the information.

USING THE Q&A STRUCTURE

You will often find question-and-answer structure texts at visitor attractions. The Visitor Centre at Chandler Gardens in Wales, Britain, receives a large number of visitors every day who are interested in learning about the gardens. The number of questions asked by the visitors – all wanting to get the most out of their visit – is very high. The communications department, realizing that there were certain questions that were being asked over and over again, produced the leaflet shown below, as a way to answer these questions as clearly, efficiently, and effectively as possible.

74 Use Q&As when you have lots of data or information to convey.

75 Aim to provide vital information and avoid straying off the point.

CHANDLER GARDENS VISITOR CENTRE
Town, County
Motorway Junction

CHANDLER GARDENS

Q. How do I visit Chandler Gardens?
A. Come to the visitor centre by exiting the motorway junction. Chandler Gardens is 6 km (4 miles) away. Follow the signposts.

Q. How much does a visit cost?
A. All tours are free of charge.

Q. What is the Tourist Visit?
A. This tour covers the biodynamic, organic vegetable and fruit gardens, nature centre, and greenhouse where we grow non-hybridized plants. You will also be shown a documentary about Chandler Gardens. The tour and film will last about an hour.

Q. What is the Special Tour?
A. This tour is open to everyone above the age of 12, in groups of a maximum of 12 people. You must book in advance.

The Special Tour will cover the same area as the Tourist Visit, plus a visit to the Natural Pesticides Building. The tour lasts about two hours.

Q. What is the Technical Tour?
A. This tour is aimed at those working as horticulturalists, gardeners, scientists, students at universities and colleges, as well as specially invited government representatives. The tour covers the inside and outside of the centre as before, with the addition of a visit to the research areas. The tour lasts about two and a half hours.

Q. What are the opening hours?
A. Opening hours vary and are as follows:
Tourist Visit:
Monday to Saturday, hourly from 8am until 4pm.
Special Tour:
Monday to Friday, at 9am and 3pm.
Technical Tour:
Monday to Friday, at 8pm and 2pm.

Chandler Gardens will be shut on Christmas Eve, Christmas Day, Boxing Day and New Year's Day.

ANTICIPATE ▶ CONCERNS
This model shows how the question-and-answer structure works in practice. Note that these questions and answers are short and succinct, covering all essential information.

IDENTIFYING PROBLEMS AND PROPOSING SOLUTIONS

If you are writing a letter in relation to a situation in deadlock, the problem-and-solution format is the best to use. This offers several solutions to the other party, allowing you both to solve the existing problem in a practical and decisive manner.

76 A friendly writing style will always be well received.

77 Be rational in your writing style and avoid emotional words and phrases.

78 Make clear suggestions, but let the recipient choose the solution.

USING THE STRATEGY

The problem-and-solution strategy is ideal for solving situations with a colleague or company, that could otherwise cause the recipient to get angry, waste time, or lose patience. With this format, you detail a summary of the problem, and end with a proposal of the possible solutions. It is a tactic that shows that you are adopting a firm approach. You are in charge. So, rather than getting emotional and becoming angry, set out your position clearly and make it clear that you will not accept any further delays or excuses.

79 Your reader does not have time to waste, so focus on the points you wish to make and keep them succinct.

▼ **GETTING RESULTS**
The diagram below shows the three parts of the problem-and-solution structure. Be objective when you use it, as there is no point in denying the facts.

Presentation of the problem	Clear analysis of possible solutions	Conclusion

PROBLEM SOLVING

It is easy to see how the problem-and-solution format can help get you out of a difficult situation. In the example detailed below, Mr. Patel bought a latest generation computer for his small business, including all the necessary peripheral equipment. He paid for the goods at the time of ordering and received them punctually. The problems began soon after installation. After two months he was still not able to:

● Connect to the Internet.
● Work for more than four hours consecutively without the operating system crashing.

Using a problem and solution structure letter, Mr. Patel obtained a satisfactory solution.

80 Write clearly, coherently, and with objectivity.

81 Present solutions with efficiency and politeness.

◀ **IDENTIFYING SOLUTIONS**
In this letter, Mr. Patel makes the problems he is experiencing quite clear and proposes definite options to resolve them. Presented with several solutions, all the supplier can really do is to accept one of them.

Today's date

Customer Services Department
Computer Company
Street Name
Big Town

Dear Sir/Madam,

The equipment I bought from your company two months ago is not working properly, and is stopping me from running my business efficiently. As the actions taken by your company have not given the desired results, I suggest that you implement one of the following three actions:

Presents the problem and details what has happened

● Give me a full refund of the computer and the peripheral equipment.
● Replace all the equipment with a new system of the same configuration that is in perfect working order.
● Arrange a visit from a qualified engineer to reinstall the equipment so that it functions properly.

Clearly defines the options available to the company

I am sure you understand that I cannot spend any more time waiting for a resolution of this problem. Please inform me which option you are going to implement by next week.

Yours faithfully,

S. Patel

Courteous tone is maintained throughout the text

USING EVERYDAY FORMATS

Achieving the right style of presentation is vital in most forms of communication. A few simple rules will help you structure effective letters, e-mails, direct mailings, and reports.

WRITING LETTERS

Letters form the basis of communication in business. A well-written, clearly laid-out letter that sticks to the point conveys the impression that your company knows what it does and does it well. Such letters are an important part of a company's public image.

82 Avoid waffle. Read through your letter and omit anything that is repetitive.

83 Check you have the right address and postcode when addressing letters.

ADDRESSING THE READER

A well-presented letter, with all the information set out clearly – and free of grammatical mistakes and spelling errors – is the minimum courtesy you should pay your recipient. Check the spelling of their name and their job title. When addressing a letter without knowledge of an individual's name, use "Dear Sir or Madam", followed by "Yours faithfully" when you sign off. If you know the recipient's name, address the letter "Dear Mr./Mrs./Ms. (add surname)" and sign off with "Yours sincerely". Do not confuse these forms of address.

THE LAYOUT OF A LETTER

- Name of the company and document number
- Date sent
- Name of the recipient
- Address of the recipient
- Subject or reference
- Body of the text
- Closing
- Signature

USING A TEMPLATE

To make your letter easy to read, follow the template when you lay the letter out. If you are writing on a company letterhead, you do not need to add your address on the right-hand side again. Align all your details on the left-hand side, starting with the date and then the name and address of the person you are writing to.

- Identify the subject on a separate line.
- Do not indent your paragraphs. Leave a line space between each new paragraph.

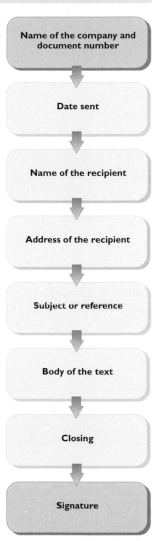

Your name and address and telephone number are written at the top

Write the name of the recipient, followed by their company name and address

Identify the subject of the letter before going into detail in the body of the letter

Range your type on the left hand side. Do not indent paragraphs

The name of the author should be followed by your job description

Catering Company
Street Name
Town
County

Today's date

Mr. Masour
Stamp Collecting Company
Street Name
Big Town

Dear Mr. Masour,

Subject: Stamp Collectors Show

During the next few days, Mr Jeremy Hyde, our Marketing Manager, will contact you to obtain the necessary details concerning the catering facilities for the above event.

Yours sincerely,

Janet Jones
Customer Services

THE RIGHT WAY ▲
Well-presented letters are clear and easy to read and understand.

ADDING TO A LETTER

When you want to attach documents or reports to your letter, or send your letter to other people as well as the recipient, you need to record this on the letter.

- When you are enclosing a document or report, write "Enc." at the bottom of your letter, two or three lines below where your job title appears.
- To inform the recipient that the letter is also being sent to others, write "cc" (carbon copy), followed by the names of the other people.

84 Use a reference code for clarity on letters about the same subject.

GOOD AND BAD STYLE

✔ 3 April 2000	✘ 3rd of April, 2000
✔ asap	✘ A.S.A.P.
✔ Page 9	✘ Page 09
✔ Yours sincerely,	✘ Yours truly,

85 Avoid casual endings such as "That's all for now".

SUBJECT AND REFERENCE CODES

Knowing how to use subject and reference codes correctly makes correspondence clearer. The subject of the letter needs to be clearly defined before the main text. When there are several letters on the same subject, a reference code is a good way to clarify which document your letter concerns. For example:
Subject: GM food products
Reference: 19/M; 19/5/2000

USING PUNCTUATION

Avoiding common errors, such as those listed below, will improve the quality of your letter.

- When abbreviating any terms, write them out first and follow with the letters in brackets. For example, United Nations (UN). The next time you refer to this, you can use the abbreviated form. However, if the organization's abbreviated form is widely known, use that instead. For example, CNN, BBC, SAS, and so on.
- Use an apostrophe to indicate the possessive, for example: Mrs. Lebrun's offices is at the end of the hall.
- Do not use an apostrophe when using a possessive pronoun, for example: The cat chased after its own tail.

ORGANIZING YOUR LETTER

Arrange your letter so that it is easier for the recipient to understand. Three general rules are listed below:

● Get straight to the point. The first paragraph should gain the attention of the reader by clearly outlining the key points of the letter.

● Repeat knowledge you share with your reader early on in your letter. However, it is important to express shared information concisely so as not to lose the reader's attention.

● Make sure that the reader knows your reasons for sending the letter and what action needs to follow.

86 Do not use "Kind regards" to end letters to people you do not know.

87 Repeat any shared knowledge in your letter as concisely as possible.

▼ GETTING IT RIGHT

The three points listed below provide the key to writing successful business letters.

| Get straight to the point | Repeat shared information | Make sure your requirements are clear |

WRITING IN A CONCISE STYLE

THE WORDY WAY	THE CONCISE WAY
"With reference to the third term of the Business Quality course, due to take place from the 26th–28th July at the Big Motel, Any Road, Phil Charles, Suzanne Page, and Lesley Storey, who were to complete the second term but could not due to their being busy with other work, we would like to request their registration for the third term of the course."	"We are applying to register Phil Charles, Suzanne Page, and Lesley Storey for the third term of the Business Quality course. The absence of these employees from the second term of the course was due to..."
"With reference to your letter request of 23/5/01 in which you asked for the exchange of air conditioners supplied by this company, we will refer to 2334/DF for authorization to substitute..."	"In connection with your letter number 2334/DF of 23/5/01 requesting the exchange of faulty air-conditioners, we will send..."

WRITING E-MAILS

E-mail is an increasingly important tool in business and accounts for a growing portion of all internal and external messages. As fast as a telephone call, e-mail can also quickly pass on large amounts of written information via attachments.

88 Overusing capital letters and bold type makes e-mails hard to read.

89 Use the reply function to respond to e-mails within 24 hours.

USING E-MAIL

Simple to use and very fast, e-mail has proved enormously useful in business. Within companies, e-mail enables instant communication with colleagues, saving quantities of paper in the process. Following a few simple guidelines makes using internal e-mails even easier. Always give your e-mail a clear "subject" heading. People receive a lot of e-mails every day, and it is helpful to be able to see which messages need to be answered immediately. Always edit what you have written before you send it. Check your grammar and make sure that the message you want to send is written in a clear, easy-to-read style.

COMPOSING E-MAILS

The speed of e-mail messages can lead to an inappropriate informality. Be careful to tailor the tone of your message to the prospective recipient and subject. Distinguish personal from business e-mails, and avoid using abbreviations, exclamation marks, and slang when writing to clients. Restrict the number of recipients to avoid overloading the system with superfluous messages. Respond to e-mails quickly, and with as brief a message as possible. If you are sending a lot of information, add file attachments to your basic message.

90 Be specific when defining the "subject" of your e-mail, making it clear to your recipient.

WRITING PRECISE E-MAILS

All your clients deserve a clear and professional response. Pay careful attention to what is being asked and respond precisely. Imprecision always doubles your workload because an incomplete answer will generate a further e-mail. However, do not lose control of the amount of information you send. If you provide more information than is requested, you may cause clients to worry needlessly about irrelevant problems. Remember, particularly when you are sending vital information, to keep a back-up copy of the e-mail so you will have a record of what has been said.

▲ USING THE RIGHT TONE
Here, the writer has used a formal style, but it can be dispensed with in e-mail, as long as the tone is not overly familiar.

POINTS TO REMEMBER

● Around 95 per cent of e-mails are jokes, gossip, unwanted advertising, and anonymous files – often containing destructive viruses. Only five per cent contain information that should really be on the network. Make sure that your e-mails fall within the latter group.

● When you have a lot of information to send, put it in attachment files. E-mail text messages should always be brief.

● Avoid using exclamation marks and abbreviations in your professional e-mails.

KEEPING YOUR MESSAGES POSITIVE AND FOCUSED

The essential ingredients for using the e-mail system successfully are keeping a positive attitude towards your client and maintaining your focus on their needs. Try to be diplomatic in your e-mails – remember nothing that a client says is directed against you personally. Avoid using capital letters to emphasize a point – they may be interpreted as an angry or negative response. Quoting from your clients' e-mails in your response is helpful. Instead of "In response to your request, we are able to tell you…", you could write: "In response to your request for information about sponsoring the artistic event, we are able to tell you…" Never be afraid to apologize if the client is right. A well-phrased apology can work to your advantage.

COMPOSING
DIRECT MAIL LETTERS

Direct mail – selling products or services to specific customers – allows you to select a target audience. Sending a carefully personalized letter is more likely to obtain a direct reply from the client, and to achieve a higher rate of response.

91 An internationally recognized good rate of response is three per cent.

92 Including a reply-paid envelope will increase the response rate.

USING DIFFERENT DIRECT MAIL METHODS

Post

Fax

E-mail

▲ GETTING RESULTS
Tailoring a mail shot to your target group will enable you to judge which medium to use. Post, fax, and e-mail can all be extremely effective.

ATTRACTING ATTENTION

When considering using direct mail, bear in mind that your first challenge is to grab the attention of your target consumer. A good direct mail needs to be interesting and convincing enough to provoke the recipient to open the envelope in the first place. Use a creative title and varied design elements such as different fonts and striking colours on the mailing envelope. If used well, these strategic elements will get the attention of your target readers and persuade them to open the envelope and see what is inside.

COMPILING DIRECT MAILS

There are five key elements involved in the structure of a successful direct mail:
● Attracting the attention of the reader by stating clearly your reason for writing.
● Arousing the reader's curiosity in the content.
● Making the product sound as attractive as possible to provoke the reader's interest.
● Using essential facts and guarantees to convince the reader of the quality of the product or service.
● Gaining action from your reader by making it clear what response you expect from them.

PROVOKING INTEREST

The principal aim of the direct mail method is to provoke the recipient's interest in the product or services on offer. Whether you are sending a simple letter or a package containing leaflets and free samples, remember to make them as compelling as you can. A covering letter should be well-written. Good design can make all the difference to an envelope, encouraging the recipient to open it. Use bullet points to highlight any benefits such as economy, guarantees of good performance, and promises of adventure.

▼ MAKING SALES

By using a simply-written covering letter with clear, objective text, the ICB company makes a convincing argument to the client. Here, the idea of economy, reliability, and smooth operation is combined with concrete benefits.

Panel Company
Street Name
Town

Today's date

Mr. Solenzky
Purchasing Manager
Building Company
Street Name
Big Town

Dear Mr. Solenzky,

Meeting your needs efficiently and providing quality and full satisfaction are our main goals at our company.

For us, this means:

● Producing panels that are durable and innovatively designed, for the best price on the market.

● Offering our clients the most convenient payment terms.

● Ensuring that our products always arrive as quickly as possible within agreed time limits.

Contact us and find out for yourself that our company is synonymous with quality and efficiency.

Yours sincerely,

Juanita Perez, Manager
Purchasing Division

---

93 Address the reader directly by using "you" to get their attention.

POINTS TO REMEMBER

● Including a freephone number or an e-mail address on your mail out makes it easy for potential clients to contact you and for them to update their details for your client mailing list.

● Without an up-to-date client list behind your direct mail shot, your marketing campaign will be less successful.

OFFERING INCENTIVES

All business communications benefit from a straightforward writing style. However, the strategies employed by direct mail are different from other types of advertising. Direct mail needs to provoke immediate action. A direct mail may offer one or more incentives such as discounts, small gifts, or attractive credit terms. It is also important to offer guarantees and user-satisfaction comments. A good client list means you can also benefit from knowing when to send the mail, such as on the client's birthday.

PRESENTING BUSINESS REPORTS

The size and format of your business report are determined by the complexity of the subject matter and your target audience. Some reports need be no longer than a single page, while the content of larger reports require more structure.

> **94** A well-presented title page on your report will create a good impression.

Company logo

Design Company

Title of the report

Recommendations for Improving Office Ergonomics at Design Company.

Author or authors of the report, plus their status

Carla Noble
Director of Human Resources
Design Company

Human Resources, Design Company

▲ THE TITLE PAGE
The title page is the first contact the reader has with the report. It should have impact and express the purpose of the document, together with the name, job title, and department of the author.

THE SUMMARY
The summary, or abstract as it is sometimes called, comprises a condensed version of the report. It states the aim of the report: what it looked at, what was found, and what action is required. Only the key points should be mentioned here.

CONTENTS PAGE
List the contents in sequence, with page number references. Provide a list of illustrations, if appropriate. Your reader will rely on this page to access the document, so make it very clear and keep the layout simple.

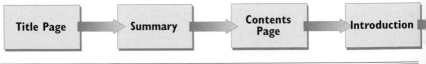

| Title Page | Summary | Contents Page | Introduction |

THE INTRODUCTION

The introduction, sometimes known as the preface, describes the background and format of the report. It should provide a broad overview of the subject, together with any necessary background details, such as the history leading up to the issue that the report addresses. The reader is told here how the discussion of the key points in the main text will be developed. If necessary, state what research methods were used.

95 Provide the key discussion points of the report in the introduction.

96 The summary is exactly that – a précis of the report's contents.

THE MAIN TEXT

This part of the report should focus on the information the reader needs to have. Here is where all the facts and evidence are laid out. Keep the development of your arguments logical, ensuring that the evidence is relevant and the arguments are clear. Present your key points first, followed by the back-up data. Order your points, making use of subheadings, bullet points, and other devices to help the reader follow your points.

CONCLUSION

The conclusion section is where you make your recommendations. It should draw upon the main text facts and your points should be both clear and precise. There should be a recommendation of action to be taken, as a result of the report's analysis of the data. However, if any issues or questions remain outstanding or unresolved, draw attention to them in the conclusion.

97 Put supporting material, such as data, in the Appendix.

◀ **THE STANDARD STRUCTURE**
Reports should contain seven elements. Sometimes the Appendices/References might not be necessary.

Main Text	➤	Conclusion	➤	Appendices/References

THE SUMMARY

The summary outlines the aims of the report before the detailed contents page. The introduction needs to give an overview of the subject matter with any relevant background details. The main text should provide facts and key points, plus supporting evidence, in a logical order. A good way of providing extra information is to expand specific topics. In your conclusion refer back to the main facts and, based on sound analysis, suggest what action to take.

98 In the report's introduction, summarize the objectives.

▼ AN IDEAL SUMMARY
A good summary will always detail the contents and main aim of the report, and highlight the key points, as shown in the example below.

THE SUMMARY

Identifies aim of the report —— Following a request made by the Board of Directors, we have produced this report with the Engineering, Marketing, and Finance Departments, with the aim of finding the best location for the new company warehouse to replace the current hangar, which is now unusable, following the fire that occurred recently.

The problem it was investigating —— Research into new locations indicates that the Greater Manchester area is the most suitable site. This conclusion is based on the following:

● The site is in close proximity to Head Office.

What came out of the research —— ● A large warehouse site is needed, as more overseas customers are buying books directly from us to take advantage of the 20 per cent discount we offer over shop prices.

● We need to keep this stock in one warehouse site situated near our Head Office.

Key points that came out of analysis —— ● Bus and train transport to the area is good.

● The road network in this area is excellent. There is also a rail freight yard, international airport, and ship canal nearby.

● Acquiring the warehouse involves a low initial investment.

● The region is densely populated and offers tax incentives for new corporations.

● There are at least three possible locations (see appendix B) that are for sale, and it seems there will be no problem recruiting local labour.

Conclusion on why the action is required —— We realize that the location of the warehouse in Greater Manchester may generate some inconvenience with distribution to the south-east of the country, but this is a minor problem compared to the overall benefits to the company of a warehouse in this area.

HOW TO PRESENT A REPORT

Once you have put together your report, you need to think about how you are going to bind it up for final presentation to make the most impact on your clients or colleagues. You may decide to use coloured paper for your report cover so that it stands out. Choose a subtle shade, as a glaring colour may give the reader the wrong impression of the report's contents.

A plastic binder with a removable spine is the simplest option. Or you may have a printer that will heat-bind it for you.

PROFESSIONAL ▶ APPEARANCE
Using coloured paper for your cover, with an eye-catching title page, looks professional.

THE APPENDICES

An appendix is not always necessary, but if there is a large amount of reference material or further information that would weigh down the main text, they are best included in an appendix at the back of the report. Appendices are ideal for any supporting facts, giving necessary explanations, or any other relevant information that will help the reader to understand the report.

99 Include analytical information and useful suggestions in your reports.

100 Present reports in an interesting way to attract the reader's attention.

101 Put any supplementary information to your report in an appendix or set of appendices.

ASSESSING WRITING SKILLS

Practice is the best way of developing and improving your writing. Analyze the statements below and evaluate your performance as a writer, selecting the options that match your level of expertise. Try to be totally honest. If your answer is "Never," put a cross through 1; if it is "Sometimes," put a cross through 2, and so on. Add up your score and then look at the Results Analysis box on page 69. Use the test to identify areas for improvement.

SCORING

1 Never

2 Sometimes

3 Often

4 Always

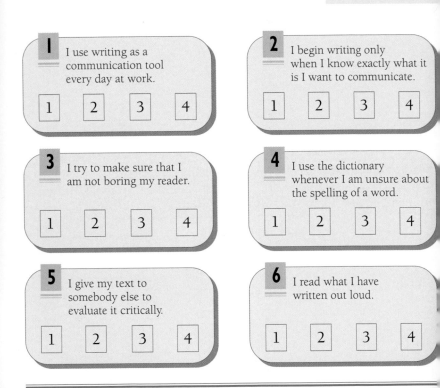

1 I use writing as a communication tool every day at work.

1 2 3 4

2 I begin writing only when I know exactly what it is I want to communicate.

1 2 3 4

3 I try to make sure that I am not boring my reader.

1 2 3 4

4 I use the dictionary whenever I am unsure about the spelling of a word.

1 2 3 4

5 I give my text to somebody else to evaluate it critically.

1 2 3 4

6 I read what I have written out loud.

1 2 3 4

7 I make my intentions totally clear to the reader.

1   2   3   4

8 I try to be pleasant and constructive when writing to people.

1   2   3   4

9 I use language that is suited to the person I am writing for.

1   2   3   4

10 I limit the information I include in my letters and documents to the essentials.

1   2   3   4

11 I respect my reader's level of knowledge of the subject I am writing about.

1   2   3   4

12 I clearly indicate the actions I recommend my reader should take.

1   2   3   4

13 I avoid the use of stilted language, slang, and unnecessary buzzwords.

1   2   3   4

14 I try not to "shout" at the reader by avoiding brash fonts and exclamation marks.

1   2   3   4

15 I always read my work afterwards to check for errors.

1   2   3   4

16 I make the information I supply as clear and easy to understand as possible.

1   2   3   4

17 I concentrate on making my text visually attractive.

1 2 3 4

18 I gather and organize my information before I start writing.

1 2 3 4

19 I identify my message first and then find the best way of explaining it.

1 2 3 4

20 I try not to write as though I am more important than my text.

1 2 3 4

21 I try to use language that is positive and optimistic – but not misleading.

1 2 3 4

22 When I reply to people, I let them know I have read their communications to me.

1 2 3 4

23 I read messages on the day I receive them and reply to them immediately.

1 2 3 4

24 I consider who should receive the information I want to pass on.

1 2 3 4

25 I try to avoid tired, overused, and clichéd phrases when writing.

1 2 3 4

26 I try to improve my knowledge through reading.

1 2 3 4

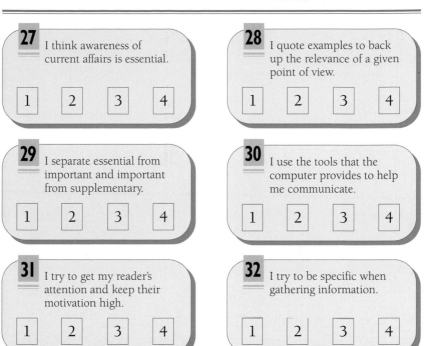

27 I think awareness of current affairs is essential.

| 1 | 2 | 3 | 4 |

28 I quote examples to back up the relevance of a given point of view.

| 1 | 2 | 3 | 4 |

29 I separate essential from important and important from supplementary.

| 1 | 2 | 3 | 4 |

30 I use the tools that the computer provides to help me communicate.

| 1 | 2 | 3 | 4 |

31 I try to get my reader's attention and keep their motivation high.

| 1 | 2 | 3 | 4 |

32 I try to be specific when gathering information.

| 1 | 2 | 3 | 4 |

RESULTS ANALYSIS

Now that you have tested yourself, add up the points you scored and compare them to the performance analysis below. Whatever your score, remember that you can always improve. Identify your weakest areas and consult the relevant sections of this book to find the practical advice and pointers that will help you improve your writing skills.

32–64: Your written communication skills could be improved. Read a little

more and practise writing daily. Compare your own documents to those of others.

65–95: Your written work has its highs and lows. Practise more, concentrate on being clear and you'll soon see the benefit.

96–128: You write very well, but remember: there is always room for improvement.

INDEX

A

abbreviations, 56
abstracts, in reports, 62
active voice, 26–27
addresses:
    addressing letters, 54
    e-mail addresses, 61
adjectives, grammar, 32, 33
adverbs, grammar, 32, 33
advice:
    accepting, 23
    asking for, 45
alphabet:
    capitalization, 33, 58, 59
    fonts, 34–35
ambiguity, 19, 29
apologies, 59
appendices, to reports, 65
archaic language, 29
assessing:
    style, 12
    skills, 66–69
attachment files, e-mails, 58, 59

B

bad communicators, 10
bad writing habits, 16
binders, reports, 65
books, reference, 14, 31
brainstorming, 50
bullet points, 61, 63
business memos, 47
business reports see reports
buzzwords, 19

C

capitalization:
    common errors, 33
    e-mails, 58, 59
charts, 37
clichés, 18
client lists, direct mail letters, 61
codes, reference, 56
colour, images, 36
communication:
    bad communicators, 10
    communicating clearly, 6–7
    communication with reader,
        40–41

good communicators, 10
computers, 9
concise writing, 24, 57
conclusions:
    business reports, 48, 63
    organizing text, 43
confusing text, 21, 25, 29
conjunctions, 33
contents pages, business reports,
    62
covers, reports, 65
creative writing, 7
criticism, accepting, 23

D

databases, 8
dictionaries, 25, 31
diplomatic style, 27
    e-mails, 59
direct mail letters, 60–61
direct mail lists, 8, 61
discriminatory style, 39
draft text, 23, 30

E

e-mails, 8, 58–59
    attachment files, 58, 59
    e-mail addresses, 61
emphasis, choosing words for, 28
executive summaries, 46

F

fake style, 20
file attachments, e-mails, 58,
    59
filing systems, 43
focused writing, 11
fonts, 34–35
formal style, 13, 29
freephone numbers, 61
full stops, 56

G

good communicators, 10
grammar, 30, 32–33
    common errors, 33
    correct usage, 33
    e-mails, 58
    parts of speech, 32

H

headings:
    business reports, 49
    coloured, 36
    e-mails, 58
    spacing and type, 36
    subheadings, 34, 49, 63

I

illustrations, 36, 37
image:
    grammatical errors and, 30
    writing style and, 12
images adding, 36, 37
incentives, direct mail letters, 61
informal style, 13
    e-mails, 58
information:
    accuracy, 14
    appendices, 65
    credibility, 6
    filing systems, 43
    question-and-answer format, 50
    research, 14, 15, 43
    using the right amount of, 15
insincerity, 19
Internet, 8, 9
    research using, 14, 31, 43
introductions:
    business reports, 63
    organizing text, 43
inverted pyramid system, 46–47

J

jargon, 16, 19
journalism, 46

K

knowing your subject, 14

L

labels, to images, 37
language:
    being self important, 19
    choosing words for emphasis, 2
    clichés, 18
    concise writing, 24, 57
    confusing text, 21, 25, 29
    defining your style, 16–21

developing vocabulary, 22
discriminatory style, 39
fake style, 20
finding the right tone, 41
grammar, 30, 32–33
insincerity, 19
jargon, 16, 19
plain English, 29
slang, 16, 58
suiting to reader, 13
using different voices, 26–29
using the right word, 25
verbosity, 18
letters (alphabet):
    capitalization, 33, 58, 59
    fonts, 34–35
letters (correspondence), 54–57
    additions to, 56
    direct mail letters, 60–61
    finding the right tone, 41
    marketing letters, 11
    organization of, 57
    planning, 23
    style of, 7
    subject and reference codes, 56
    templates, 7, 55

M

mail shots, 60–61
making a thesaurus, 31
marketing letters, 11
meetings, minutes, 13
memos, 7, 47
minutes, of meetings, 13

N

negative writing, 38, 39
nouns, grammar, 32, 33

O

old-fashioned styles, 7
outlines, 44

P

page layout:
    business reports, 49
    letter templates, 55
    spacing and type, 36
paragraphs:
    planning, 42
    structure, 44
parts of speech, grammar, 32–33
passive voice, 26–27
photos, 36
plain English, 29

planning, 13, 15, 42
positive writing, 38–39
prefaces, to reports, 63
preparation, 12–15
prepositions, grammar, 32, 33
presentation, 34–37
    charts and tables, 37
    fonts, 34–35
    images, 36–37
    reports, 65
presentations, structure, 48
problem-and-solution strategy, 52–53
professional style, 6
pronouns, grammar, 32, 33
proposals, 23
punctuation, 33, 56
puns, 25
pyramid structure, 46–47

Q

question-and-answer format, 50–51

R

reading:
    aloud, 32
    widely, 22
reference books, 14, 31
reference codes, on letters, 56
repetition, avoiding, 25
reports, 23, 48–49, 62–65
    appendices, 65
    conclusion, 48, 63
    contents page, 62
    introduction, 63
    main text, 63, 64
    presentation, 62–65
    structure, 48, 62–63
    summary, 48, 62, 64
    title page, 62
research, 14, 15, 43
    using Internet, 14, 31, 43
revising text, 45
rewriting text, 45

S

sans serif fonts, 34
schematics, 9
script fonts, 35
self-importance, writing styles, 19, 20
sentences:
    active voice, 26–27
    passive voice, 26–27

composition, 24–25
construction, 16
reading aloud, 32
syntax, 32
serif fonts, 34
slang, 16, 58
solutions, problem vs. solution strategy, 52–53
spacing headings, 36
spelling mistakes, 30
statistics, charts and tables, 37
structuring writing, 15, 42–53
style, defining, 16–21
subheadings:
    business reports, 49, 63
    fonts, 34
subject headings:
    e-mails, 58
    letters, 56
subtlety, 38
summary, business reports, 48, 62, 64
syntax, 32

T

tables, 37
targeting material, 9
tautology, 25
technical language, 21
technology, 8–9
telephone, freephone numbers, 61
templates, letters, 7, 55
thesaurus, making one, 31
title pages, business reports, 62
tone, reader communication, 41
typefaces, 34–35
typewriters, 8

V

verbosity, 18
verbs:
    emphatic language, 28
    grammar, 32, 33
visitor attractions, using question-and-answer format, 51
visual skills, 9
vocabulary see language
voice:
    active voice, 26–27
    passive voice, 26–27

W

word-processing packages, fonts, 35
words see language

ACKNOWLEDGMENTS

PUBLISHER'S ACKNOWLEDGMENTS

Dorling Kindersley would like to thank the following for their help in
producing this book:

Editorial assistance Alison Bolus, Amy Corzine, Richard Gilbert, Nigel Ritchie;
Indexer Hilary Bird; **Translator** Michael Salvage, Multilingua, Guildford, UK;
Jacket editor Beth Apple; **Jacket designer** Sophia M.T.T.

Main photographer Steve Gorton; **Other photographers** Andy Crawford, Tim Ridley;
Photographer's assistants Andy Komorowski, Lee Walsh, Nici Harper, Nick Goodall, Sarah Ashun;
Photographic co-ordinator Laura Watson.

Photographic models Angela Cameron, Ann Winterborn, Ben Glickman, Carole Evans, Chantell Newell,
Cornel John, Daniel Stevens, Felicity Crowe, Fiona Terry, Frankie Mayers, Gilbert Wu, Ian Midson, James
Kearns, Jane Cooke, Janey Madlani, John Gillard, Karen Murray, Kiran Shah, Kuo Kang Chen, Lois
Sharland, Lynne Staff, Maggie Mant, Marian Broderick, Mary-Jane Robinson, Miles Elliot, Mutsumi Niwa,
Patrick Dobbs, Peter Taylor, Philip Argent, Pipa Oakes, Richard Hill, Roberto Costa, Sasha Heseltine, Sotiris
Melioumis, Suki Tan, Ted Nixon, Teresa Woodward, Vosjava Fahkro, Wendy Yun, Zahid Malik.

Picture Research Samantha Nunn.

PICTURE CREDITS

Powerstock Photolibrary/Zefa: Norman Jung 4-5.

All other images © Dorling Kindersley

For further information see: **www.dkimages.com**